SUPER
CHEF

The Cooking of
THAILAND

This book is dedicated to Dr. Archie Karfly.

This author's sincere gratitude to Peter Mavrikis, Michelle Bisson, Kay Petronio, and Anahid Hamparian.

Published by Marshall Cavendish Benchmark
An imprint of Marshall Cavendish Corporation
All rights reserved.

Text © 2012 by Matthew Locricchio

Food photographs © 2012 Jack McConnell, McConnell, McNamara & Company
Map © 2012 by Mike Reagan
Illustrations by Janet Hamlin
Illustrations © 2012 by Marshall Cavendish Corporation

This publication represents the opinions and views of the author based on Matthew Locricchio's personal experience, knowledge, and research. The information in this book serves as a general guide only. The author and publisher have used their best efforts in preparing this book and disclaim liability rising directly and indirectly from the use and application of this book.

Other Marshall Cavendish Offices:
Marshall Cavendish International (Asia) Private Limited, 1 New Industrial Road, Singapore 536196 • Marshall Cavendish International (Thailand) Co Ltd. 253 Asoke, 12th Flr, Sukhumvit 21 Road, Klongtoey Nua, Wattana, Bangkok 10110, Thailand • Marshall Cavendish (Malaysia) Sdn Bhd, Times Subang, Lot 46, Subang Hi-Tech Industrial Park, Batu Tiga, 40000 Shah Alam, Selangor Darul Ehsan, Malaysia

Marshall Cavendish is a trademark of Times Publishing Limited
All websites were available and accurate when this book was sent to press.

Library of Congress Cataloging-in-Publication Data

Locricchio, Matthew.
The cooking of Thailand / Matthew Locricchio.
p. cm. — (Superchef—2nd ed.)
 Summary: "Introduces the different culinary regions of Thailand and presents many kinds of recipes for traditional Thai dishes"— Provided by publisher.
 Includes bibliographical references and index.
ISBN 978-1-60870-556-6 (print) — ISBN 978-1-60870-744-7 (ebook)
1. Cooking, Thai. 2. Cookbooks. I. Title. II. Series.
TX724.5.T5L62 2012
641.59593—dc22
        2011005594

Editor: Peter Mavrikis
Publisher: Michelle Bisson
Art Director: Anahid Hamparian
Series design by Kay Petronio
Art direction for food photography by Matthew Locricchio
Food styling by Marie Hirschfeld and Matthew Locricchio

Photo Credits: Prisma/Superstock: 14; Steve Vidler/Superstock: 18; Axiom Photographic Limited/ Superstock: 19; Matthew Locricchio: 40, 60; Photka/Fotolia: 89; volff/Fotolia: 89; Photka/Fotolia: 90; S©Tomboy2290/Fotolia: 90; Le Do/Fotolia: 91; zhongliang li/Fotolia: 92; LanaLanglois/Fotolia: 92; Peter Jameson: 96.

Printed in Malaysia (T)
135642

SUPER
CHEF

The Cooking of

THAILAND

second edition
Matthew Locricchio

with photos by Jack McConnell

Marshall Cavendish
Benchmark
New York

Contents

Dear Reader,

I can't think of a better way to learn about a culture first-hand than to cook and savor its cuisine. Understanding the breadth of Italian pasta varieties, or Greek phyllo specialties and greens dishes, of Chinese dumplings, Indian curries, Thai spice blends, and more helps us understand something about the geography, history, and soul of a country.

My first memories of food come from my own family, of Sunday meals that lasted half the day and holidays that required a week of cooking. There was a rhythm to the dishes we ate depending on the time of year, with specific sweets for Christmas, breads for New Year's, and the vegan fare my grandmother would prepare as we fasted for Easter. For me, food became synonymous with both communicating and sharing. The dinner table was a time of talking about the issues of the day. The holidays and impromptu visits by family and friends became reason to put a little something on the table for others to enjoy. Those are important lessons to carry through life and they are learned young. As a kid I always helped in the kitchen, regardless of whether I wanted to or not! Thanks to that I learned to cook fairly young, and by the time I was a teenager, I was inviting my friends over to try my own creations.

Young people today are much more food savvy than I was way back in the 1960s and 1970s. Teenagers have a much broader experience with ethnic foods than I ever did. There was no such thing as organic food when I was growing up. We also did not have access to the constant stream of information available today. Ironically, with the overabundance of information out there on food, there is very little real knowledge about how to cook simple, healthy, good food.

The Superchef series of cookbooks aims to do just that and in the process show young people that the world is, indeed, one delicious kitchen where many different cooking traditions flourish.

Cooking is an art, but it's also more than that. People can live without music, paintings, sculpture, and literature, but we can't live without food! So, enjoy the process, but better yet, enjoy sharing it with others.

Diane Kochilas

Consulting chef
Pylos Restaurant, NYC

Diane Kochilas is a chef, author, and teacher. She has published over a dozen cookbooks including, *The Food and Wine of Greece*, *The Greek Vegetarian*, *Meze*, *The Glorious Foods of Greece*, *Mediterranean Grilling* and more. Diane has also made numerous television and radio appearances, and runs a cooking school focusing on traditional Greek recipes, as well as the culture of Greece. To learn more about Diane, go to www.dianekochilas.com.

From the Author

Welcome to the second edition of Superchef. When we first created this series of cookbooks our goal was to introduce new cooks to traditional yet tantalizing recipes from around the world, adapted to work in your kitchen. That goal has not changed.

Young chefs like yourself who discovered Superchef have been learning to cook international recipes with family and friends ever since. The world of satisfying recipes, along with the basic principles of kitchen safety, food handling, and common-sense nutrition is what made Superchef so popular when it was first introduced. Those same goals hold true with the new edition.

Learning to master authentic international recipes and sharing them with family and friends is the motivation behind these cookbooks. This edition offers the invitation to new cooks as well as old to step into the kitchen and start cooking. Within this complete series you will find classic recipes from eight different countries. The recipes are not necessarily all low-fat or low-calorie, but they are all healthful. Even if you are a vegetarian, you will find recipes without meat or with suggestions to make the dish meatless.

Superchef can change the way you feel about cooking. You can learn to make authentic and delicious dishes from recipes that have been tested by young cooks in kitchens like yours. The recipes range from very basic to challenging. The instructions take you through the preparation of each dish step by step. Once you learn the basic techniques of the recipes, you will understand the principles of cooking fresh food successfully.

There is no better way to get to know people than to share a meal with them. Today, more than ever, it is essential to understand the many cultures that inhabit our planet. One way to really learn about a country is to know how its food tastes. Cooking is the one thing we all have in common. You can prepare a recipe in your kitchen and know that somewhere, perhaps many thousands of miles away, that same dish is probably being prepared in the country where it originated.

Every day in the United States we are reminded of our multicultural richness just by the foods available to us. The delicious result of that abundance is that American cooking has developed into one of the most diverse and appealing cuisines on the planet.

Learning to cook is one of the most important things anybody can do. Cooking skills stay with you your entire life and it sure is fun. Learning to cook takes practice, patience, and common sense, but it's not nuclear science. Cooking certainly has its rewards. Just the simple act of preparing food can lift your spirits. Nothing brings family and friends together better than cooking and then sharing the meal you've made. It can be fun, and you get to eat your mistakes. It can even lead to a high-paying career. Most importantly, you can be proud to say, "Oh, glad you liked it. I did it myself."

Happy cooking!

Matthew Locricchio

Matthew Locricchio

Before You Begin

A Word about Safety

Safety and common sense are the two most important ingredients in any recipe. Before you begin to make the recipes in this book, take a few minutes to master some simple kitchen safety rules.

Ask an adult to be your assistant chef. To ensure your safety, some steps in a recipe are best done with the help of an adult, like handling pots of boiling water or hot cooking oils. Good cooking is about teamwork. With an adult assistant to help, you've got the makings of a perfect team.

Read the entire recipe before you start to prepare it, and have a clear understanding of how the recipe works. If something is not clear, ask your teammate to explain it.

Dress the part of a chef. Wear an apron. Tie back long hair so that it's out of your food and away from open flames. Why not do what a chef does and wear a clean hat to cover your hair!

Always start with clean hands and a clean kitchen before you begin any recipe. Always wash your hands again after handling raw meat, poultry, or fish. Leave the kitchen clean when you're done.

Pot holders and hot pads are your friends. The hands they save may be your own. Use them only if they are dry. Using wet holders on a hot pot can cause a serious burn!

Keep the handles of the pots and pans turned toward the middle of the stove. That way you won't accidentally hit them and knock over pots of hot food. Always use pot holders to open or move a pan on the stove or in the oven.

⬤ **Remember to turn off the stove and oven when you are finished cooking.** Sounds like a simple idea, but it's easy to forget.

Be Sharp about Knives

⬤ A simple rule about knife safety is that your hands work as a team. One hand grips the handle and operates the knife while the other guides the food you are cutting. The hand holding the food should never come close to the blade of the knife. Keep the fingertips that hold the food slightly curved and out of the path of the blade, and use your thumb to keep the food steady. Go slowly. There is no reason to rush.

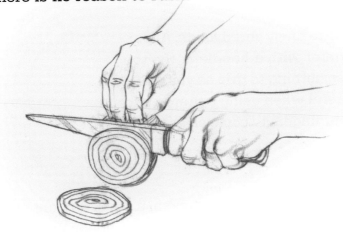

⬤ Always hold the knife handle with dry hands. If your hands are wet, the knife might slip.

⬤ Work on a cutting board, never a tabletop or countertop.

⬤ Never place sharp knives in a sink full of soapy water, where they could be hidden from view. Someone reaching into the water might get hurt.

⬤ Take good care of your knives. Good chef knives should be washed by hand, never in a dishwasher.

Cooking Terms

Thai cooking blends subtle flavors, fresh ingredients, and visual appeal with the pure pleasure of eating. Even though Thai cuisine shares many common elements with neighboring India, Vietnam, and Malaysia, the nation's cooks have developed their own cooking techniques and recipes. Here are a few culinary techniques to help you master the cooking of Thailand.

Grate

To grate means to finely shred foods. A four-sided metal grater with a handle at the top will give you something to grip as you work. Always be careful when using a grater, and don't allow your fingers to come close to the grating surface.

Sauté

To lightly fry food in a small amount of fat, butter, or oil, while stirring with a spoon or spatula.

Simmer

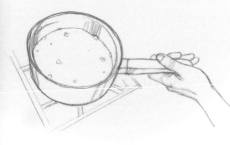

To cook food in a liquid at just below the boiling point. Gentle bubbles roll lazily to the top of the liquid that is simmering.

Skim

Fats or impurities will rise to the surface of simmering or boiling soups and sauces. Skimming removes these unwanted residues while also reducing fat and enriching flavor. Use a large metal spoon or small ladle to scoop off the top layer.

Stir-fry

Stir-frying is a simple cooking technique. But a successful stir-fry is not something that just happens. It takes planning and preparation.

Here Are a Few Tips

- Cut the main ingredients into fairly small pieces as described in the recipe. If you cut them so they are about the same size, everything will cook more evenly and be done at the same time.

- After you have cut or sliced the various ingredients, line them up near the wok in the order that you will use them. When you start to stir-fry, there is no time to run around the kitchen looking for tools and ingredients.

- Preheat your wok for about 30 seconds on high or medium-high heat to make sure the surface is evenly heated.

- Add the oil and tip the wok slightly from side to side to evenly coat the cooking surface.

- When cooking the ingredients, use a long-handled metal spoon or Chinese spatula to move them. The important thing to remember is to spread them evenly across the wok's cooking surface. That way more of the ingredients are in contact with the hot surface and foods will cook uniformly.

- Once the food is cooked remove it from the wok to its serving dish.

- To clean the wok, rinse it with hot water (no soap) and wipe the inside with a clean damp cloth to remove stuck-on food. Rinse again and return the wok to the stove. Heat the wok over medium heat and, as it is beginning to dry, wipe it with a paper towel to finish drying it. Turn the heat off. Let it cool, and then pour in a tiny amount of oil, rubbing the surface with a clean paper towel to coat the wok. Then your wok will be ready for the next time you need it.

The Regions of Thailand and How They Taste

For the people of Thailand, it is important that every aspect of life—even hard work—have a sense of *sanuk* or "fun." This is especially true with Thai cooking, since sanuk is always present in the preparation and the enjoyment of meals. Maybe that is why food is such a key part of many Thai celebrations.

Located in Southeast Asia, Thailand has been at the crossroad of many culinary influences. India, China, Malaysia, and Vietnam have all contributed to the range of exciting flavors found in Thai cooking. Even the cuisines of southern Europe and the Middle East have left their mark. Sugar, eggs, tomatoes, asparagus, peas, carrots, and chile peppers, to name a few, were all introduced to Thailand by its bordering nations. So what is it about Thai cooking that makes it different from its neighbors? The answer is the taste. The flavors created in Thai food go beyond the classic tastes of Southeast Asia—hot, sweet, spicy, sour, and salty. Thai cooks blend ingredients such as curry paste, Thai fish sauce, shrimp paste, coconut, palm sugar, and hot chile peppers into the complex, fragrant, and layered flavors that make their dishes distinctly Thai. For a country that is a little smaller than the state of Texas, and with a population of about 66 million people, Thailand's national cuisine enjoys an ever-growing popularity around the world. The cooking of Thailand has developed and thrived by opening its kitchens to the influences of the flavors of neighboring cultures.

Thai restaurants have popped up in cities across the globe. But nowhere is Thai food more appreciated than in the nation that started it all. For the people of Thailand, sharing food with family and friends is one of the greatest pleasures of life. To them, a meal is much more than a collection of ingredients or a blending of flavors. The real essence of a dish is in its presentation. Thai cooks take great pride in their creations. They strongly believe that the appeal of a dish should go beyond its taste. A Thai meal should be beautiful to look at as well. Delicately carved

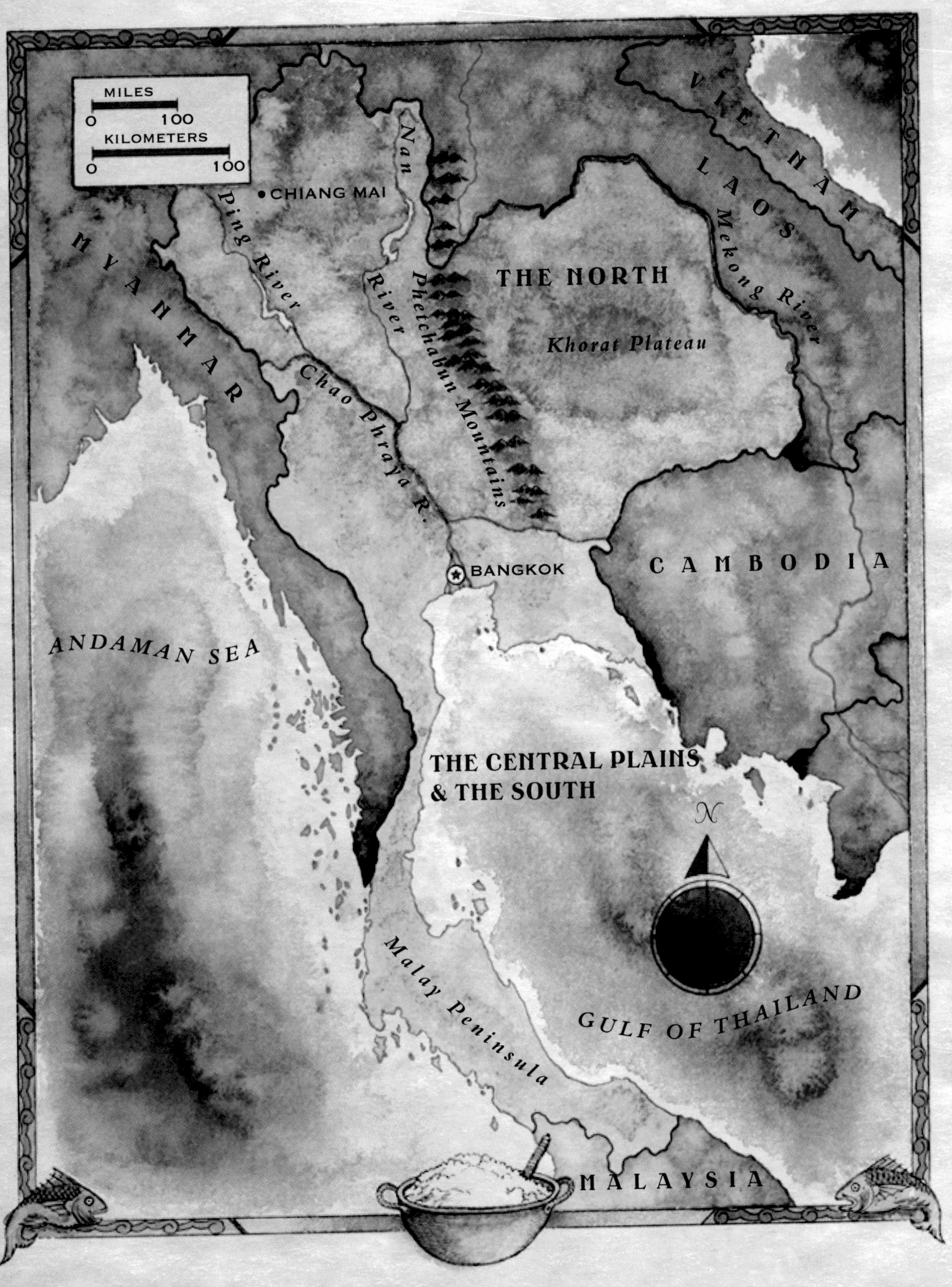

MILES

0   100

KILOMETERS

0   100

VIETNAM

LAOS

•CHIANG MAI

THE NORTH

Khorat Plateau

Mekong River

MYANMAR

Ping River

Nan River

Phetchabun Mountains

Chao Phraya R.

★ BANGKOK

CAMBODIA

ANDAMAN SEA

THE CENTRAL PLAINS
& THE SOUTH

N

Malay Peninsula

GULF OF THAILAND

MALAYSIA

vegetables and fruit flowers grace dishes that are served to guests and family alike. The garnish that is used to accent a dish is always fresh and colorful, to add that signature touch to a memorable meal.

The best way to discover what makes Thai cooking so appealing is to look more closely at its culinary parts. For this purpose, we will divide Thailand into two regions, the north and then the area commonly referred to as the central plains and the south. Along the way we will stop and explore the role of street food—foods prepared by vendors mostly in cities but in the surrounding countryside as well—which is a major part of the cooking of Thailand.

The North

Northern Thailand, bordered by Myanmar, Laos, and Cambodia, is a region rich in history, culture, and natural beauty. Thailand's climate is regulated by the tropical monsoons of Southeast Asia. The rains generally begin in May and can last until September. They leave behind a lush landscape, teeming with plant life. The north is the country's most heavily forested area. The creation of national parks and preserves has helped return the region to its once dense groves of evergreen, hardwood, and teak trees. Mountainous and rugged, composed of sweeping upland valleys, sparkling lakes, and remarkable rivers, the north is enchanting not only for its natural beauty, but also for the mysterious temple ruins and

A farmer checks the progress of recently planted rice in a paddy field in northern Thailand.

spectacular ancient monuments found throughout the region. Hill tribes live in villages along the northern border with Myanmar. These peoples, including the Lawa, the Kui, and the Karen, can trace their cultural roots back thousands of years. Today many still live close to the land, and the corn and rice they grow is used in countless local recipes. Many people regard the north as the original home of Thailand's culture and traditions are still preserved to this day through language, dress, and cuisine.

Chiang Mai, the nation's northernmost province, is a blend of the contemporary and the traditional. It is home to some of the country's most beautiful temple ruins dating back thousands of years. Yet the modern world is evident as well in the bustling city also called Chiang Mai. In spite of its contemporary pace, Chiang Mai is regarded as one of Thailand's most appealing cities to live in and remains a popular spot for tourists who seek out its unique combination of the past and the present.

The cooking of the north features some unique combinations and is generally not quite as spicy as the cooking in central and southern Thailand. Pork is a key ingredient there, and the region is known for its sausages, as well as a sweet pork dish braised in soy sauce and sugar. Local ginger, peppercorns, chiles, green beans, bamboo shoots, sweet peppers, and Thai basil combine to make a savory local vegetable curry. The region is also famous for its hospitality. In front of local houses, a small raised platform covered with a slanted roof is a common sight. A jar of cool water and a ladle are often waiting underneath in case a passing traveler is in need of a refreshing drink.

As you move east, the Khorat Plateau, a vast tableland, rises some 650 to 1,000 feet (200 to 300 meters) above sea level. The land there is bordered by the Phetchabun Mountains, which have kept the region, known as Isaan, isolated. Travel, especially in the rainy season, in this remote region is often difficult. But the trek is more than worth it. Isaan offers the curious traveler famous ruins, emerald-green monsoon forests, and outstanding views of the Mekong River from the low-lying hills. The people there speak Lao or Thai dialects, and the cooking reflects the influence of Laos to the north. Fresh herbs are used to enliven grilled and roasted foods. The heavy and frequent rains make preserving foods a necessity, such as a combination of fresh cabbage, radishes, and shallots in a sweet vinegar syrup. Another northern dish that is famous all over Thailand is a spicy chicken salad with chiles, mint, and garlic. Versions of this salad are served on Thai tables everywhere and are popular items often sold from vendors' carts.

Traditional markets of the north and northeast supply residents with fresh fruits, vegetables, fish, and meats. They can be as simple as a solitary vendor selling produce on the side of the road or as busy as a crowded urban market. In the large markets, concrete tables are filled daily with the freshest foods, which are quickly snatched up by discriminating Thai cooks. These markets are open usually in the mornings and afternoons to make it convenient for the Thai shopper to find the best ingredients just before it is time to cook dinner.

Street vendors are another common sight in the north, cooking and selling fresh foods made to order. The province of Si Saket is famous for the grilled chicken sold from carts and food stalls there. Marinated chicken is split into small sections, flattened, laid in a bamboo frame, and then tied to hold it in place. The meat is then grilled over an open fire. The lines of people waiting to buy this chicken offer strong testimony to the popularity of this tasty dish.

Green papaya salad is also popular in Isaan. The customer tells the vendor the exact ingredients to add, as well as how hot or sweet to make it. The vendor then pounds the ingredients together in a clay bowl called a mortar. Using a wooden mallet called a pestle, a distinctive tinkling sound rings out as the wooden pestle strikes the clay. The result of all this labor is a crunchy, spicy, and healthful salad.

For a taste of northern Thailand try: Curried Vegetables; Hot and Sour Shrimp Soup; Spicy Chicken Salad; Sweet Pork; Green Papaya Salad; and Grilled Chicken dishes.

The Central Plains and The South

Central Thailand has been inhabited for more than 2,000 years. Historically it is the site of Thailand's main trading routes. Merchants from around the world came for centuries to buy and sell silks, spices, gems, lamps, exotic lumber, and ivory. Cities and towns sprang up along the riverbanks. Their distinctive houses are still built on stilts to protect them from flooding.

The majestic Nan and Ping rivers flow southward into the central plains. Eventually these waterways join forces to become the Chao Phraya River, also known as the "river of kings." The land that runs along the Chao Phraya is rich and fertile, making the central plains the "rice bowl" of Thailand. The ideal climate and abundant rainfall have also helped to make this area the most densely populated region in Thailand.

The rich soil of the central plains produces not only rice, but mangoes, sugarcane, limes, lemongrass, eggplants, bamboo shoots, chile peppers, bananas, pineapples, and coconuts. The area's agricultural seasons are simply defined as wet and dry. When it is too dry for rice, peanuts, corn, and taro are planted in the fields. But no matter the season, central Thailand produces a wealth of fresh foods. This is only one of the reasons this region is regarded as the home of "classic" or traditional Thai cooking. Local cooks take full advantage of the diversity of ingredients, and take great pride in their style of local cooking.

One unique feature of the central valley is its vast network of human-made canals. They flow from the various local rivers and their tributaries. They supply irrigation to farmers and provide habitat for an assortment of freshwater fish and shrimp. Fresh shrimp pulled from local waters often find their way into a hot and sour soup popular across Thailand. The easy-to-make recipe of shrimp in green curry combines fresh shrimp with green curry paste and coconut milk. It is sold by vendors on busy canal streets to shoppers looking for fresh fish, produce, and even barges loaded with rice.

The hundreds of miles of canals that cut through the region are also home to a unique Thai institution—the floating market. Customers and sellers alike arrive in boats usually in the early morning. Instead of pushing a grocery cart like in a traditional Western supermarket, shoppers paddle along selecting the freshest picks of the day. Boats selling savory noodle dishes and other delights are always anchored close by, just in case shoppers get hungry.

Lying near the southern coast, Bangkok, the nation's capital, is one of the region's main attractions. With its approximately 6 million people, it is home to more than 10 percent of the country's population. It is a city brimming with treasures—from its solid gold Buddha to its glittering spires and stately teak buildings. With its architecture, music, history, spectacular skyline, and shopping, it comes as no surprise that Bangkok is a magnet for tourists. It is also considered one of the most exciting food cities in the world, and for good reason. Regional culinary influences from every corner of the country, and from neighboring Vietnam, Laos, Malaysia, and India, come together in the city's lively cuisine. Visitors and locals alike find it irresistible.

Another appealing aspect of Bangkok cuisine adds a regal dimension to Thai cooking. Until recently, royal Thai cooking was restricted

to the royal family. Around 1968, King Bhumibol Adulyadej decided it was time to share his royal palate with the rest of the nation. Cookbooks that held the court's recipes were published and made available to all. Today royal recipes are not only a part of everyday Thai cooking, they have also found their way onto the world's table. Dishes such as coconut rice and a rich chicken and bamboo shoot curry certainly demand royal attention wherever they are served. The royals even had dishes created in their honor. For example, King Rama VII had a dish created to celebrate his great equestrian skills. Pineapple chunks and orange slices act as the horse, and a sweet and spicy filling of ground nuts and pork create the rider in a festive, tasty appetizer.

Bangkok locals may dine out four to five times a day, just because they enjoy it so much. Restaurants are not the only place to savor delicious meals, however. Street food is a cuisine all its own in Thailand. Carts and food stalls (complete with stools), roadside drive-ins, and even "noodle boats," which sail along the many canals from behind the skyscrapers of Bangkok, all offer an endless assortment of authentic Thai food. Eating plays such an important role in the daily life of Bangkok that it is hard to visit any part of town without finding yourself within a few feet of a restaurant or street vendor's cart.

Just south of Bangkok, at the beginning of the Malay Peninsula, is the province of Phetburi. Its ancient temples are one of the area's main draws. But there is another reason visitors seek out this part of Thailand. The local coconut custard is almost as famous. The palms that grow here produce a wealth of sugar, and the local cooks are renowned for their desserts. The baked coconut custard from the region has become so popular that it is now sold in shops across Thailand. A moist cake made from bananas and coconut is also a specialty of the region.

Farther south is the province of Phuket, which is also Thailand's largest island. Its beautiful beaches, limestone cliffs, breathtaking sunsets, and great seafood dishes have earned it the nickname "the pearl of the south." Surrounded by the waters of the Andaman Sea, Phuket cooks are also known for another creation not found in many other regions of Thailand. Breads called *roti* are hugely popular and have been dubbed "the croissant of Thailand." Rolled thin, then lightly fried, this sweet crispy bread is perfect to enjoy with the fiery local yellow curries loaded with turmeric and an abundance of chile peppers. Local limes are blended into limeade, the perfect drink to cool the curries' fire.

To experience a taste of the central plains and the south of Thailand try: Coconut Rice; Galloping Horses; Chicken in Red Curry with Bamboo Shoots; Shrimp in Green Curry; Chicken and Coconut Milk Soup; Baked Coconut Custard; and Banana Cake.

The cooking of Thailand offers the promise of truly exciting cuisine. Once you start preparing the recipes in this book, you will discover why Thai cooking is so highly regarded among those who love great food. As they would say in Thailand, *"Churn rub pro than mak mak na kha,"* or "make yourself at home and eat all you like."

Food stall vendors dish out some lucky shopper's lunch.

Soups and Stocks

n left: hot and sour soup, shrimp soup
chicken and coconut milk soup

Chicken Stock
Nam Tom Gai

The Thai cook uses this simple combination of ingredients to produce a rich and flavorful stock. You can always buy canned broth as a substitute, but once you taste your own homemade chicken stock, you might conclude that the canned version simply doesn't compare.

Makes about ½ gallon

Ingredients

2 ½ pounds chicken wings
(preferably organic)

1-inch-piece fresh ginger

1 to 2 garlic cloves

5 or 6 stems cilantro

6 cups cold water

On your mark, get set . . .

- Rinse the chicken wings under cold water, drain, and place them in a large pot.

- Lay the ginger on a cutting board and slightly crush it. Add it to the pot.

- Slightly crush the garlic by laying the flat side of a chef's knife on the clove and pressing evenly to break open the skin.

- Add the crushed garlic, with its skin, to the pot.

- Rinse the cilantro to remove any dirt and add it to the pot.

Cook!

- Place the pot on the stove and add the water. Bring to a boil, uncovered, over high heat. This will take 20 to 30 minutes.

- As the liquid comes to a boil, use a large spoon to skim off any foam or impurities that rise to the top.

- Cover the pot, leaving the lid slightly ajar. Reduce the heat to simmer and let cook for 1 ½ to 2 hours.

- With the help of your adult assistant, strain the broth through a colander into a heatproof bowl or pan and set aside.

- When the cooked ingredients have cooled, discard.

- Let the stock cool for 20 minutes and then refrigerate or freeze it. After it has chilled, any fat in the stock will collect at the top and should be removed and discarded.

- Store the completed stock in the refrigerator for up to 4 days or for 3 months in the freezer.

- Never thaw frozen stock at room temperature. Instead thaw it overnight in the refrigerator or in a pan on the stove over low heat.

Hot and Sour Shrimp Soup
Tom Yam Goon

This soup successfully blends salty, hot, and sour flavors into one of the dishes most often associated with Thai cooking. Hot and sour shrimp soup is a popular dish in Bangkok, but it actually originated in the more coastal parts of the country where shrimp are so plentiful. When shopping for this recipe, look for fresh shrimp or prawns in their shells. You may use frozen shrimp as well, just make sure to thaw them completely.

Serves 4 to 6

Ingredients

1 ½ pounds fresh or thawed, frozen medium shrimp

1 teaspoon sea salt or kosher salt

1 cup cold water

1 to 2 stalks lemongrass or one recipe lemongrass substitute (page 45)

1-inch-thick slice fresh ginger or galangal

6 small white button, oyster, or straw mushrooms

8 to 10 stems cilantro

3 to 5 serrano or jalapeño chiles, depending on taste

2 limes

4 cups homemade chicken stock (page 22) or canned low-sodium chicken broth

1 ½ tablespoons Thai fish sauce

On your mark . . .

- Carefully peel off the shells and the tails of the shrimp but don't discard them. Set them aside for later use.

- Remove the vein from the shrimp.

- To do this, lay the shrimp on a cutting board. Using a paring knife, make a slight cut about ¼ inch deep, starting at the widest end or the top of the shrimp.

- As you cut, you will see a black vein.

- Rinse the shrimp under cold running water, then pull out and discard the vein.

- Repeat with the rest of the shrimp.

- Place the shrimp in a large bowl and add the salt and the cup of cold water. Toss the shrimp with a spoon a few times to help dissolve the salt and then refrigerate them.

Get set . . .

- If using lemongrass, cut off the root end of the stalk.

- Peel and discard the tough outer layers until you expose the lighter purple-colored inner stalk.

- Slice a 2-inch piece of the stalk into thin slivers. Lemongrass is tough and stringy, so slice it carefully. Measure ¼ cup and set aside.

- Peel the outer skin from the ginger or galangal with a vegetable peeler.

- Lay the peeled slice flat on a cutting board and crush it with the flat side of a chef's knife. Chop it finely, measure 1 tablespoon, and set aside.

- Brush off any dirt from the mushrooms with a soft, dry brush or damp paper towel. Cut the mushrooms into thin slices, measure ¼ cup, and set aside.

- Remove the leaves from the cilantro and set aside.

- Finely chop the stems of the cilantro, measure 1 tablespoon, and set aside. Roughly chop the cilantro leaves and set aside.

- Slip on a pair of latex kitchen gloves. Remove the stem from the chiles and cut them in half.

- Remove the seeds by running the chile pepper under cold running water. Scrape out any seeds with the tip of a teaspoon and discard.

- Slice the chiles into thin pieces, place in a small bowl, and set aside. Rinse, dry, and remove the gloves.

- Wash the limes. Using a vegetable peeler, remove four ½-inch-wide by 1 ½-inch-long sections of the outer peel, or zest of the lime. Be careful not to cut too deeply into the skin. You want only the green skin and not the white pith underneath.

- Cut the limes in half and remove the juice by either squeezing the limes by hand or using a citrus juicer or reamer. Measure 3 tablespoons and set aside.

Cook!

- Drain the shrimp, reserving the water it has been soaking in.

- Pour the soaking water into a medium-size pan, add the shells and tails, and bring to a boil over medium-high heat. Lower the heat to medium, and cook for 6 to 8 minutes. The liquid should be reddish in color. This is the shrimp stock.

- Strain the stock over a bowl, then press against the shells with the back of a large spoon to remove any remaining liquid. Discard the shells.

- In a large pot, combine the shrimp and chicken stock. Add the chopped lemongrass (if using), the ginger, and fish sauce. Bring to a boil over high heat.

- Add the mushrooms, shrimp, and lime zest.

- Reduce the heat to medium and cook for 3 to 4 minutes, or until the shrimp turn pink and are just cooked through.

- Remove the pan from the heat and add the lime juice.

- If using the lemongrass substitute, add it into the soup.

- Add the chopped chiles, cilantro leaves and stems, and give the soup a stir.

- Ladle it into individual bowls and serve hot.

Chef's Tip

Tell your guests that even though sliced lemongrass looks like green onion, it is not recommended that it be eaten. Thai cooks use lemongrass for flavor in their cooking, but they eat around it in the dishes they prepare.

Chicken and Coconut Milk Soup *Tom Kha Gai*

This rich and spicy soup comes from the north and bears the influence of neighboring Laos. Traditionally this soup is made with galangal, a member of the ginger family that is an essential ingredient in traditional Thai cooking. This version uses more commonly available ginger with very satisfying results. But if you are lucky enough to have an Asian grocery in your area, use galangal, which can be purchased fresh or frozen.

Serves 4 to 6

Ingredients

6 ounces boneless skinless chicken breasts or thighs, preferably organic

4 ounces oyster or cremini mushrooms

1 stalk lemongrass or lemongrass substitute (page 45)

2 shallots

2 garlic cloves

8 to 10 sprigs cilantro

1 ½-inch-thick slice fresh ginger or galangal

3 to 5 serrano chiles, depending on taste

1 lime

3 cups chicken stock (page 22) or canned low-sodium chicken broth

2 cups canned unsweetened coconut milk

1 teaspoon salt

1 teaspoon light brown sugar

2 tablespoons Thai fish sauce

cilantro leaves, for garnish

On your mark . . .

- Wash the chicken pieces and pat dry with a paper towel.

- Slice the chicken into long, thin slices ½ inch wide, and then cut the slices into ¼-inch chunks.

- Place the chicken pieces in a bowl and refrigerate.

- Brush off any dirt from the outside of the mushrooms using a soft, dry brush or damp paper towel. If using oyster mushrooms, cut off the tough stems and discard.

- Tear the remainder of the mushrooms into small pieces and place in a bowl. If using cremini mushrooms, slice them into ¼-inch-thick slices and place in a bowl. Set the mushrooms aside.

Get set . . .

- If using lemongrass, cut off the exposed root end of the stalk. Peel and discard the tough outer layers until you expose the inner stalk.

- Cut about 3 to 4 inches of the stalk into thin slices. Lemongrass is tough and stringy, so slice it carefully. Measure 1 tablespoon and set aside.

- Slightly crush the shallots, then the garlic.

- Remove the skin from both, finely chop, measure 2 tablespoons combined, and set aside.

- Wash the cilantro to remove any dirt. Pluck off the leaves and set aside for garnishing the soup.

- Finely chop the cilantro stems, measure 1 tablespoon, and set aside.

- Peel the outer skin from the ginger or galangal and discard.

- Cut the ginger or galangal into thin slices and set aside.

- Slip on a pair of kitchen gloves. Cut the chiles in half and remove the stem.

- Rinse the chiles under cold running water and scrape out and discard the seeds.

- Chop the chiles into small pieces and set aside.

- Rinse, dry, and remove the gloves.

- Using a vegetable peeler, slice off four ½-inch-wide by 1-inch-long sections of the outer peel, or zest, of the lime.

- Be careful not to cut too deeply into the skin. You want only the green part. Set the lime peels aside.

- Cut the lime in half, squeeze out the juice, measure 1 tablespoon, and set aside.

Cook!

- Combine the chicken stock and coconut milk in a 6- to 8-quart pan, add the salt and sugar, cover the pan with the lid slightly ajar, and bring to a boil over medium-high heat.

- Remove the lid, add the lemongrass, garlic-and-shallot mixture, cilantro stems, chopped chiles, ginger, and lime zest.

- Reduce the heat to low and cook uncovered for 1 to 2 minutes.

- Add the chicken and mushrooms and cook for 4 to 5 minutes, or until the chicken is cooked through.

- Turn off the heat.

- Add the fish sauce, the reserved lime juice, and the cilantro leaves.

- If using the lemongrass substitute, add it at this time.

- Stir well to combine the ingredients, ladle the soup into individual serving bowls or a large tureen, and serve hot.

Clockwise from upper left: spicy chicken salad, pickled vegetables, cucumber relish, and green papaya salad.

Salads,
Relishes, and
Appetizers

Spicy Chicken Salad
Laab Gai

The name of this salad means "good fortune," and for that reason it is a popular dish at parties and celebrations. Spicy chicken salad, a recipe that dates back centuries, originated in Isaan, in northern Thailand. Today *laab gai* has become popular all over the country. Thai cooks know that, once the salad is prepared, they will have the good fortune of tasting it.

Serves 6

Ingredients

3 shallots

1 lime

3 green onions

4 to 5 sprigs fresh mint

6 to 8 Boston lettuce leaves

1 small cucumber

1 ripe medium tomato

2 tablespoons unsalted peanuts

1 pound ground chicken meat

2 tablespoons Thai fish sauce

2 teaspoons light brown sugar

1 to 2 teaspoons chili powder, depending on taste

On your mark, get set . . .

- Peel the skin off the shallot, finely chop, measure 2 tablespoons, and set aside.

- Cut the lime in half and squeeze the juice into a small bowl. Measure 2 tablespoons and set aside.

- Wash the green onions, remove and discard any dark or discolored outer leaves, chop into small pieces, measure ¼ cup, and set aside.

- Wash the mint and shake off the excess water. Then roll the sprigs in a paper towel to blot them dry.

- Remove the leaves from the stems. Discard the stems, roughly chop or tear the leaves into small pieces, and set aside.

- Wash the lettuce leaves, pat dry with a paper towel, and set aside.

- Wash, peel, and slice the cucumber into thin slices and set aside.

- Remove the stem circle from the tomato, cut the tomato in half and then into small chunks, and set aside.

- Roughly chop the peanuts and set aside.

Cook!

- Place the chicken in a 3-quart pan along with the fish sauce, reserved lime juice, sugar, and chili powder and place over medium heat.

- Cook the chicken, stirring with a large slotted spoon to break up the meat and ensure even cooking. This will take 6 to 8 minutes. The chicken is cooked when it is no longer pink.

- If the chicken seems too dry, you can add 2 tablespoons of water.

- Remove the chicken to a large bowl with the slotted spoon.

- Add the reserved chopped shallots, green onions, peanuts, and mint leaves and toss together to coat the chicken.

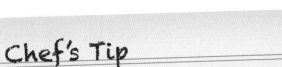

- Tear the lettuce leaves into bite-size pieces.

- Arrange the lettuce, cucumber slices, and tomatoes on a serving platter.

- Add the chicken to the center of the platter and serve.

Chef's Tip

If you can't find ground chicken, you can grind it yourself in a food processor. Ask your adult assistant to help with this step. Cut 1 pound of skinless, boneless chicken breasts into 1-inch cubes and process until the texture resembles ground beef.

Cucumber Relish
Ar-jad Tan-gwa

Serves 6

Ingredients

1 medium cucumber

3 shallots

1-inch-thick slice fresh ginger

3 to 4 sprigs cilantro

1 red or green jalapeño chile (optional)

4 tablespoons white or coconut vinegar

4 tablespoons water

3 tablespoons granulated sugar

¼ teaspoon salt

On your mark, get set . . .

- Wash and peel the cucumber. Cut the cucumber in half lengthwise, then into quarters lengthwise, and then into ½-inch slices. Measure ½ to ¾ cup, place in bowl, and set aside.

- Peel the skin off the shallots, slice thinly, and set aside. Peel the outer skin from the ginger and discard. Cut the ginger into thin slices. Finely chop or mince the ginger strips into tiny pieces, measure 1 tablespoon, and set aside.

- Rinse the cilantro, then shake off the excess water. Remove the leaves, chop, and set aside. Discard the stems.

- Wearing kitchen gloves, remove the stem and cut the chile in half. Rinse the chile under running water, scrape and discard the seeds.

- Cut the chile into thin slices and set aside. Rinse, dry, and remove the gloves.

Cook!

- In a small saucepan, combine the vinegar, water, sugar, and salt.

- Bring the pan to a boil over medium-high heat and stir occasionally to dissolve the sugar.

- Cook for 1 to 2 minutes, remove from the heat, and cool. This is the syrup.

- Add the cucumber to a bowl with the shallots, ginger, cilantro, and chile slices, if using.

- Add the syrup to the cucumber mixture, toss, and serve.

Green Papaya Salad
Som Tam

This zesty salad originally comes from the northern city of Chiang Mai but is known all over Thailand. Traditionally *som tam* is made in a tall ceramic mortar called *krok din*. Ingredients are pounded together, as customers instruct the vendors on the level of heat and sweetness to put in. The racket, created by vendors working feverishly to serve their hungry customers, is a familiar sound ringing out in the local streets. When shopping for this recipe, look for papaya that is green and hard. That is how you'll know it's not yet ripe. This version offers an alternative to green papaya if none happens to be available in your area.

Serves 6 to 8

Ingredients

1 medium unripe green papaya or 4 carrots and ¼ small head of green cabbage

1 to 2 garlic cloves

1 to 2 serrano, red jalapeño, or Thai chiles (depending on taste)

8 whole cherry tomatoes or 1 ripe medium whole tomato

½ cup fresh green beans (about 3 ounces)

2 limes

2 tablespoons unsalted roasted peanuts

½ teaspoon salt

1 tablespoon granulated sugar

2 tablespoons Thai fish sauce

lettuce leaves, cucumber slices, carrot sticks, and shredded cabbage, for serving

On your mark . . .

- Peel the papaya with a vegetable peeler and cut in half. Scrape out the seeds.
- Rinse the papaya halves and pat dry with a paper towel.
- Grate the papaya into a bowl using the largest holes on a four-sided grater.
- Measure ¾ to 1 cup, place in a hand strainer, and gently press with the back of a spoon to remove any excess liquid.

- If substituting carrots and cabbage for the papaya, wash, peel, and cut off the tops of the carrots.

- Remove any dark or discolored leaves from the cabbage.

- Shred the carrots using the largest holes on a four-sided grater, measure ½ cup, and place in a small bowl.

- Shred the cabbage like the carrots, measure ½ cup, combine with the carrots, and set aside.

Get set . . .

- Slightly crush the garlic by laying the flat side of a chef's knife on the clove and pressing evenly to break open the skin.

- Remove the skin and cut the garlic into quarters and add to a stainless-steel bowl large enough to hold all the ingredients.

- Slip on a pair of kitchen gloves. Remove the stem and cut the chile in half.

- To remove the seeds, rinse the chiles under cold running water and scrape out and discard the seeds.

- Chop the chiles into small pieces and add to the bowl.

- Rinse, dry, and remove the gloves.

- Wash the tomatoes, then cut in half if using cherry tomatoes, or into 4 wedges if using a whole tomato. Add them to the bowl.

- Wash the green beans, remove the stems and tips, cut into 2-inch pieces, and set aside.

- Cut the limes in half, squeeze the juice into a small bowl, measure 2 tablespoons, and set aside.

Cook!

- Sprinkle the salt and sugar over the garlic, chiles, and tomatoes in the large bowl.

- Using a metal soup ladle, begin gently

mashing the garlic, chiles, tomatoes, salt, and sugar, until they are crushed and combined.

- Add the green beans, a few at a time, and continue to mash until they are combined as well. This may take a few minutes, so be patient. It isn't necessary to overly mash the ingredients for this salad, just crush things into bite-size chunks.

- Add the peanuts and continue mashing.

- Add the papaya or carrot-cabbage combination and mash together.

- Mix in the fish sauce and the reserved lime juice with a spoon, and the salad is ready to serve.

- Prepare a serving platter with freshly washed lettuce leaves, cucumber slices, shredded cabbage, and carrots sticks.

- Spoon the salad onto the lettuce leaves and serve at once.

Galloping Horses *Mah Haw*

Here is a recipe created to celebrate the legendary equestrian skills of Thailand's King Rama VII's. The chefs in the royal court, in Bangkok, came up with a beautiful and mouth-watering recipe. The fruit is the horse and the filling is the rider. The recipe combines the best of Thai flavors like, sweet, crunchy, and spicy, and a real eye-catching design. Thai cooks love to present their dishes looking beautiful. Though it takes a little patience to put this appetizer together, it will be a tribute to your guests when you serve this dish at the start of your next Thai meal.

Makes 32 pieces

Ingredients

1 fresh pineapple or 1 20-ounce can of sliced pineapple

1 navel (seedless) orange

1 small bunch of cilantro (4 to 5 sprigs)

1 to 2 red jalapeño or serrano chiles or to taste

1 clove of garlic

2 tablespoons cold water

1 tablespoon peanut or canola oil

½ pound ground pork or ground turkey

2 tablespoons crunchy peanut butter

1 tablespoon Thai fish sauce

2 tablespoons light brown or turbinado (raw) sugar

On your mark . . .

If using fresh pineapple:

- Ask your adult assistant to cut off the top and about 1 inch of the bottom of the pineapple and discard. Using a sharp knife, cut off the outer skin of the pineapple and discard. Cut the pineapple in half lengthwise.

- Stand the pineapple up and cut out the tough core at the center and discard. Cut the pineapple into four ½–inch thick slices. Cut each slice into 4 pieces.

- You will need 16 pieces of pineapple. Save any leftover pineapple for snacking or another recipe.

If using canned pineapple:

- Drain the liquid from the can. Carefully remove 4 slices of pineapple.

- Lay the slices on a clean cutting board or tray and pat them dry with paper towels.

- Cut each slice into quarters. You will need 16 slices of pineapple.

- Cover the pineapple with wax paper or plastic wrap and refrigerate while you prepare the rest of the recipe.

- Wash and peel the orange. Remove as much of the white outer skin as you can. Cut the oranges into four ½-inch-thick slices. Cut the slices in 4 pieces. You will need 16 slices of oranges. Cover the slices with wax paper or plastic wrap and set aside.

Get set. . .

- Wash the cilantro to remove any dirt. Remove the leaves from 3 or 4 of the sprigs for garnish. Pluck off the leaves from the stems and discard the stems. Set aside ½ the leaves for garnish. Finely chop the remaining leaves, measure 1 tablespoon, and set aside.

- Slip on a pair of kitchen gloves.

- Cut the chiles in half and remove the stem.

- Rinse the chiles under cold running water and scrape out and discard the seeds.

- Lay the chiles cut side down on a clean cutting board, cut into small pieces, and set aside.

- Rinse, dry, and remove the gloves.

- Slightly crush the garlic by laying the flat side of a chef's knife on the clove and pressing evenly to break open the skin. Remove the skin and finely chop the garlic and set aside.

- In a small bowl, combine the water and peanut butter until smooth and set aside.

Cook!

- Heat the oil in a 9-to 10-inch skillet over medium-high heat until hot, but not smoking.

- Add the chopped garlic and ground meat.

- Cook for 3 to 4 minutes or until the meat has lost its pink color. Stir constantly to break up the chunks of meat and to prevent sticking.

- Reduce the heat to medium and add the peanut butter, fish sauce, sugar, and chopped chiles to the skillet.

- Stir well to combine all the ingredients into a smooth, chunky paste. Cook for 3 to 4 minutes or until slightly thickened. This is the filling.

- Remove the filling to a bowl, add the chopped cilantro and mix well. Allow the filling to cool completely. It can be refrigerated for up to 1 hour.

- Arrange the fruit slices alternating with one pineapple and one orange slice on a serving tray.

- Lay a cilantro leaf on each piece of fruit.

- Top the fruit with some of the filling.

- Serve hot or at room temperature.

Chef's Tip

Fresh pineapple is sold in some supermarkets already peeled, cored, and ready to slice.

Pickled Vegetables
Pak Dong

Here is a simple recipe from Bangkok that transforms everyday vegetables into a crunchy and light dish.

Serves 6

Ingredients

1 small head red or green cabbage

3 green onions

1 large cucumber

3 to 4 radishes

1 to 2 red or green jalapeño chiles

1 cup rice or white vinegar

1 cup water

1 cup granulated sugar

2 tablespoons salt

On your mark, get set . . .

- Peel the darker outer leaves from the cabbage and cut the head in half. Refrigerate one half to use at another time.

- Grate the remaining cabbage on a four-sided grater into thin shreds. Measure about 4 cups and place in a glass or stainless-steel bowl.

- Wash the green onions, remove and discard any dark or discolored outer leaves, cut the onions into ¼-inch slices, and add to the cabbage.

- Peel the cucumber and cut in half lengthwise.

- Lay the cucumber, flat side down, on a cutting board and cut into ½-inch-wide slices.

- Cut the cucumber slices into small cubes, measure 2 cups, and add to the cabbage.

- Wash the radishes and cut off the tops. Cut the radishes into thin slices, measure ¾ to 1 cup, and add to the rest of the vegetables.

- Slip on a pair of kitchen gloves. Remove the stem and cut the chiles in half.

- To remove the seeds, rinse the chiles under cold running water and scrape out the seeds with the tip of a teaspoon. Discard the seeds.

- Chop the chiles into thin slices and add to the bowl. Rinse, dry, and remove the gloves.

Cook!

- In a medium saucepan, combine the vinegar, water, sugar, and salt. Bring to a boil over medium-high heat for 1 to 2 minutes. Let cool for about 20 minutes.

- Pour the cooled liquid over the vegetables and let them stand in the liquid for at least 30 minutes before serving, or overnight.

- Serve with shrimp in coconut cream (page 71) or alongside meat or fish recipes.

Lemongrass Substitute

Lemongrass is a key ingredient in Thai cooking, and its flavor is distinctive. If you are unable to find fresh lemongrass for the recipes in this book, here is a substitute. Add it to your recipe just before serving to keep the flavor at its peak. Though there is no substitute for the real flavor of lemongrass, this alternative will come pretty close.

Makes about 2 teaspoons

Ingredients

6 to 8 mint leaves

2 teaspoons lime juice

¼ teaspoon granulated sugar

¼ teaspoon chopped fresh ginger

On your mark, get set, mix!

- Cut the lime in half and squeeze the juice. Measure 2 teaspoons and pour into a small bowl.

- Add the sugar and stir well to dissolve the sugar.

- Remove the peel from a small piece of ginger.

- Finely chop the ginger, measure ¼ teaspoon, and add to the bowl.

- Wash the mint and shake off any excess water. Roll the sprigs in a paper towel to absorb the remaining water. Unroll the sprigs and remove the leaves from the stems. Discard the stems. Finely chop the mint leaves and place them in the bowl with the rest of the ingredients.

- Let stand for 10 minutes.

- Add to the recipe just before serving.

Stir-fried Thai noodles.

Rice and Noodles

Coconut Rice *Khoa Mun*

Coconut rice takes everyday rice and makes it sweet and soothing. In addition to dressing up your Thai meals, you may find yourself serving it alongside many of your Western recipes as well.

Serves 6

Ingredients

1 ½ cups jasmine or other long-grain white rice

2 cups canned unsweetened coconut milk, regular or lite (1 14-ounce can)

1 ¼ cups water

1 tablespoon granulated sugar

pinch salt

On your mark, get set . . .

- Place the rice in a bowl.
- Fill the bowl with cold water and, using your very clean hands, swirl the rice around to help remove the starch.
- Carefully pour off the water, but not the rice.
- Repeat this step 3 times.
- Drain the rice in a metal strainer and shake off any excess water.

Cook!

- Pour the coconut milk, water, sugar, and salt into a 4-quart pan.
- Add the rice and stir well to combine all the ingredients and help dissolve the sugar and salt.
- Bring the rice to a boil over medium-high heat. Cover the pan, reduce the heat to simmer, and cook for 20 minutes.
- Turn off the heat and let the pan stand, undisturbed, for at least 5 minutes before serving.

White Rice *Khao Suoy*

The first thing the Thai cook does to begin preparing a meal is to cook the rice. Rice is the most important part of any Thai meal. In Thailand the word for rice is *khao*, the same word that is used to mean "food." Rice demands great respect in Thailand, and the rice of choice is jasmine. Jasmine rice has both a nutty flavor and a sweet fragrance that alerts everyone in the household that something delicious is being prepared and soon it will be mealtime. Look for Thai jasmine or basmati rice for the recipe below.

Serves 4 to 6

Ingredients

2 ½ cups Thai jasmine or basmati rice
(1 pound)

3 ½ cups cold water

On your mark, get set . . .

- Place the rice in a bowl.
- Fill the bowl with cold water and, using your very clean hands, swirl the rice around to help remove the starch.
- Carefully pour off the water, but not the rice.
- Repeat this step 3 times.
- Drain the rice in a metal strainer and shake off any excess water.

Cook!

- Place the rice in a 3- to 4-quart pan. Add the water.
- Bring the water and rice to a boil over high heat. Cover the pan, reduce the temperature to simmer, and cook for 20 minutes.
- Turn off the heat and let the pan rest, undisturbed, for 10 minutes.
- Remove the lid, fluff the rice with a fork, and serve.

Stir-Fried Thai Noodles
Pad Thai

Pad Thai noodles are probably the best-known dish in Thai cooking. For many, this dish was their first taste of Thai cooking. The recipe was introduced to Thai cuisine in the seventeenth century by Chinese chefs who cooked for Thailand's royal court. The dish, with its blend of sweet, sour, and salty flavors, was so popular that it quickly found its way into most Thai kitchens. There was one slight change, though—the recipe was altered to include Thai and not Chinese ingredients. Today this famous dish is enjoyed across the country and in most of the world. This version comes from the busy restaurants of Bangkok.

Serves 4

Ingredients

THE NOODLES

1 7-ounce package dried rice noodles
   or rice sticks

THE SAUCE

2 limes

¼ cup Thai fish sauce

¼ cup dark brown sugar

2 tablespoons rice wine or white vinegar

2 tablespoons Worcestershire sauce

1 teaspoon chili powder or paprika

1 tablespoon ketchup

THE STIR-FRY

½ pound fresh large or fully thawed,
   frozen shrimp (10 to 12)

2 garlic cloves

2 green onions

5 or 6 sprigs cilantro

1 small red bell pepper

½ cup roasted unsalted peanuts

¼ pound bean sprouts (about 3 cups)

1 ounce firm tofu

3 tablespoons vegetable or peanut oil

2 large eggs, slightly beaten

On your mark . . .

- Place the rice noodles in a large bowl.
- Cover the noodles with warm water and push them down with your fingers to completely submerge. Let soak for 1 hour.

- If you are short on time, cover the noodles with very hot tap water or boiling water and let them soak for 5 to 7 minutes.
- After the noodles have soaked and softened, drain them in a colander, place them in a bowl, and cover them with a clean damp towel or plastic wrap to keep them moist.
- To make the sauce, cut one of the limes in half, squeeze the juice, measure 1 tablespoon, and place in a small bowl.
- Add the rest of the ingredients for the sauce to the bowl, mix well, and set aside.
- Cut the remaining lime into wedges and set aside to use for garnish.

Get set . . .

- Carefully peel off the shells and the tails of the shrimp and discard.
- Remove the veins from the shrimp.
- To do this, lay the shrimp on a cutting board. Using a paring knife, make a slight cut about ¼ inch deep, starting at the widest end, or the top, of the shrimp.
- Gently open the cut and you will see a black vein. Rinse the shrimp under cold running water, then pull out and discard the vein. Repeat with the rest of the shrimp.
- Cut each shrimp into 3 pieces, place in a large bowl, and refrigerate.
- Slightly crush the garlic by laying the flat side of a chef's knife on the clove and pressing evenly to break open the skin.
- Remove the skin and chop the garlic, measure 2 tablespoons, and set aside.
- Wash the green onions and remove and discard any dark or discolored outer leaves. Chop the white part and 3 inches of the green tops into ¼-inch pieces and set aside.
- Wash the cilantro, shake off the excess water, dry by rolling it in a paper towel, then set aside for garnish.
- Wash the bell pepper and cut it in half. Remove the seeds, slice the pepper lengthwise into thin slices, measure ½ cup, and set aside.

- Coarsely chop the peanuts and set aside.

- Rinse the bean sprouts in a colander, shake off the excess water, measure 2 ½ cups, and set aside. Save the other ½ cup of sprouts for garnish.

- Cut the tofu into ½-inch-thick slices, then cut the slices into ¼-inch cubes.

- Measure ½ cup, and place close to the stove, along with the oil, garlic, shrimp pieces, sauce, green onions, bell pepper, chopped peanuts, eggs, and bean sprouts.

Cook!

- Heat a wok or 12-inch frying pan over medium-high heat.

- Add the oil and heat for 30 seconds.

- Add the garlic and stir-fry for about 30 to 40 seconds.

- Add the shrimp and tofu, spread them evenly around the cooking surface in a single layer, and let them cook without stirring for about 1 minute.

- Stir-fry for another 3 to 4 minutes, or until the shrimp turn pink and are cooked through and the tofu is lightly browned.

- Add the noodles, and stir-fry until they are evenly coated with the oil. Take your time and be careful not to let the noodles spill over the side of the pan or wok.

- Add the sauce and stir-fry for 3 to 4 minutes, or until almost all the liquid has been absorbed into the noodles.

- Push the noodles aside to open up the center of the wok or frying pan.

- Add the beaten eggs and cook without stirring for about 1 minute, or until the eggs begin to set.

- Add the peanuts, bean sprouts, green onions, and bell pepper, and stir-fry until all the ingredients are well combined and the eggs are broken up and cooked. This will take a few minutes, so be patient.

- Serve hot on a large platter and garnish with the extra bean sprouts, lime wedges, and cilantro sprigs.

Clockwise from upper right: curried vegetables, shrimp in coconut cream, chicken in red curry with bamboo shoots, grilled chicken with sweet-heat sauce, and coconut rice.

Curries and Main Dishes

Chicken in Red Curry with Bamboo Shoots
Gaeng Paedt Gai Nor-mai

During the rainy season, bamboo crops up in abundance across the fertile flatlands of central Thailand. The young shoots are harvested and used in many dishes. Chicken in red curry with bamboo shoots is one of the most popular. Though fresh bamboo shoots are used most commonly in Thai kitchens, canned ones offer an easy alternative. This simple recipe will give you a chance to try out the red curry paste (page 63).

Serves 6

Ingredients

10 ounces skinless, boneless chicken breasts, preferably organic

1 8-ounce can sliced bamboo shoots or hearts of palm

1 red jalapeño chile pepper (optional)

1 bunch green or Thai purple basil

1 lime

1 can unsweetened coconut milk

1 to 2 tablespoons red curry paste, according to taste

1 ½ tablespoons granulated sugar

2 tablespoons Thai fish sauce

¼ teaspoon salt

On your mark, get set . . .

- Rinse the chicken breasts under cold water and pat them dry with a paper towel.

- Lay the chicken breast on a cutting board and slice it lengthwise into 1-inch-thick slices.

- Cut the slices into ½-inch cubes, measure 1 ½ to 2 cups, and refrigerate.

- Wash the cutting board, the knife, and your hands with hot soapy water and dry thoroughly.

- Open the bamboo shoots or hearts of palm and drain in a colander. Rinse thoroughly with cold water and set aside.

- If using the jalapeño, slip on a pair of kitchen gloves.

- Remove the stem and cut the jalapeño in half.

- To remove the seeds, rinse the chile under cold running water and scrape out the seeds with the tip of a teaspoon and discard.

- Chop the chile peppers into small pieces and set aside.

- Rinse, dry, and remove the gloves.

- Wash the basil and shake off the excess liquid. Pull the leaves off the stems, then wrap in paper towels to remove the last traces of water. Remove the leaves and discard the stems.

- Save 4 or 5 of the nicest basil leaves for garnish, tear the rest of the leaves in two or three pieces each, measure 1 cup, and set aside.

- Wash the lime and, using a vegetable peeler, remove four 1-inch-wide strips of the outer peel. Be careful not to cut too deeply into the lime skin. You only want the green skin and not the white pith underneath.

- Lay the pieces of peel on top of each other and cut them into thin strips.

- Chop the strips into small pieces, measure 1 teaspoon, and set aside. Save the rest of the lime for another recipe.

Cook!

- Open the can of coconut milk, being careful not to shake it.

- Use a teaspoon to remove the thickened coconut cream from the top of the can, measure ¾ cup, and place it in a wok or 4-quart saucepan.

- The coconut milk that remains at the bottom of the can will be lighter in color and thinner than the cream. Set it aside for the moment.

- Add the curry paste to the coconut cream and bring to a gentle boil over medium heat. Cook for 2 minutes, stirring occasionally to combine.

- Add the chicken pieces and stir-fry for 5 to 7 minutes, or until the chicken is white and cooked through, with no pink inside.

- Add the rest of the coconut milk, lime peel, sugar, bamboo shoots, chile, basil leaves, fish sauce, and salt.

- Stir well to combine all the ingredients and stir-fry for 5 minutes.

- Serve hot with rice, using the extra basil leaves as garnish.

Shrimp in Green Curry
Gaeng Keao wan Kung

Green curry is the most recognizable of Thai curries and maybe you might be familiar with it from seeing it on Thai menus. Green curry is typical of dishes from the central plains region. Green curry paste has become so popular today that it is usually found in most supermarkets in the Asian foods section. This dish is easy to put together, once you've prepared the ingredients, and can be done at the last minute. Serve it with white rice, (page 50)—and you will see how simple and unforgettable Thai cooking can be.

Serves 4

Ingredients

1 pound extra-large shrimp

5 to 6 stems fresh cilantro

1-inch piece fresh ginger or galangal

1 lime

2 to 3 serrano or jalapeño chile peppers
   depending on taste

2 tablespoons green curry paste

2 13 ½ ounce cans of unsweetened coconut
   milk, regular

1 tablespoon Thai fish sauce

5 to 6 basil leaves for garnish

white rice for serving (recipe page 50)

On your mark . . .

- Carefully peel off the shells and the tails of the shrimp and discard.
- Remove the vein from the shrimp. To do this, lay the shrimp on a cutting board. Using a paring knife, make a slight cut about ¼ inch deep, starting at the widest end or the top of the shrimp.
- As you cut, you will see a black vein. Rinse the shrimp under cold running water, then pull out and discard the vein.
- Repeat with the rest of the shrimp.
- Place the shrimp in a large bowl and refrigerate them while you prepare the rest of the ingredients.

Get set . . .

- Peel the outer skin from the ginger or galangal with a vegetable peeler.
- Lay the peeled slice flat on a cutting board and crush it with the flat side of a chef's knife. Chop it finely, measure 1 tablespoon, and set aside.
- Wash the lime and, using a vegetable peeler, remove four 1-inch-wide strips of the outer peel. Be careful not to cut too deeply into the lime skin. You only want the green skin and not the white pith underneath.
- Lay the pieces of peel on top of each other and cut them into thin strips.
- Chop the strips into small pieces, measure 1 to 2 teaspoons, and set aside.
- Cut the lime in half, squeeze the juice, and set aside.
- Slip on a pair of kitchen gloves.
- Remove the stem and cut the jalapeños in half.
- To remove the seeds, rinse the chile under cold running water and scrape out the seeds with the tip of a teaspoon and discard.
- Chop the chiles into small pieces and set aside.
- Rinse, dry, and remove the gloves.

Cook!

- Open the cans of coconut milk, being careful not to shake them.

- Use a teaspoon to remove the thickened coconut cream from the top of the cans, measure 1 cup, and place it in a wok or 4-quart saucepan.

- The coconut milk that remains at the bottom of the cans will be lighter in color and thinner than the cream. Set it aside for the moment.

- Add the green curry paste to the wok or saucepan with the coconut cream and stir well to combine. Cook over medium heat for 3 or 4 minutes or until the curry and coconut milk come to a soft boil.

- Add the shrimp and cook for 2 to 3 minutes, or until the shrimp just turns pink.

- Add the rest of the coconut milk, lime peel and juice, chopped cilantro, chopped chiles, and fish sauce.

- Stir well to combine all the ingredients.

- Cook for 3 minutes.

- Rinse the basil leaves, pat dry, and tear them in half.

- Serve hot with rice and garnish with the basil leaves.

Red Curry Paste *Prik Gaeng*

The distinctive taste of some Thai dishes comes from the full flavor of curry pastes. Red curry paste is one of the milder pastes Thai cooks use. It is also one of the most versatile. Traditionally curry paste is made by pounding all the ingredients together with a stone mortar and pestle until smooth. Each ingredient is added one at a time and ground with the previous ingredients until all are combined into a smooth paste. It is time consuming, but the results are delicious. For greater convenience, however, you can grind excellent pastes in a food processor, with the help of your adult assistant, of course. Curry pastes are also available in supermarkets and specialty food stores, but most Thai cooks prefer to make them at home. Why not give it a try?

Makes ¾ cup

Ingredients

6 dried New Mexico, long red, or arbol chiles

4 garlic cloves

3 shallots

1-inch-piece fresh ginger or galangal

1 stalk lemongrass or lemongrass substitute (page 45)

6 to 8 stems cilantro

1 teaspoon shrimp paste or bean paste/miso (optional)

1 ½ teaspoons ground coriander

½ teaspoon ground cumin

1 teaspoon salt

8 black, white, or green whole peppercorns

On your mark . . .

- Slip on a pair of latex kitchen gloves.
- Cut the stem off the dried chiles and slit the chiles in half lengthwise. Open and remove the seeds and the light-colored membrane from the inside and discard.
- Cut the chiles into 1-inch-wide slices and place in a small bowl.
- Add 1 cup warm (not hot) water and let the chiles soak while you prepare the rest of the ingredients.

Get set . . .

- Slightly crush the garlic by laying the flat side of a chef's knife on the clove and pressing evenly to break open the skin.

- Remove the skin, chop the garlic, measure 1 ½ to 2 tablespoons, and set aside.

- Repeat this step with the shallots. Measure 1 to 1 ½ tablespoons and add to the garlic. Place the mixture in the bottom of a food processor with its metal blade already in place.

- Peel the outer skin from the ginger or galangal and discard.

- Cut the ginger or galangal into thin slices. Stack the slices on top of each other and then cut them into long strips. Finely chop or mince the ginger strips into tiny pieces, measure 1 tablespoon, and add to the food processor.

- If using lemongrass, cut off the root end of the stalk. Peel and discard the tough outer layers until you expose the lighter-colored inner stalk.

- Starting at the bottom of the stalk, slice 2 inches of it into thin slivers. Lemongrass is tough and stringy, so slice it carefully. Measure 2 tablespoons and add to the processor.

- Wash the cilantro to remove any dirt.

- Shake off the excess water and roll the cilantro in a paper towel to absorb any remaining water.

- Remove the leaves from the stems and store for another recipe; you will just be using the stems.

- Finely chop or mince the stems, measure 2 teaspoons, and add to the processor as well.

- Add the chiles to the processor along with ½ cup of the chile-soaking liquid.

- Add the shrimp or bean paste, if using, the ground coriander, cumin, salt, peppercorns, and lemongrass substitute, if using.

Grind!

- With the lid in place, process for 30 seconds.

- Open the lid and, using a rubber spatula, scrape down the sides of the bowl.

- Return the lid and process for 1 minute, or until a smooth red paste is formed.

- Carefully scrape the paste into a small bowl, being very careful of the blade.

- The curry paste will keep for 1 week refrigerated in an airtight container or for up to 3 months frozen.

Chef's Tip

Shrimp paste is available in Asian specialty markets and some supermarkets. To make the red curry paste vegetarian, substitute miso for the shrimp paste, or omit the shrimp paste altogether.

Curried Vegetables
Phak Ruam Mitr

The northern region of Thailand is home to this tantalizing and flavorful stir-fry. Vegetables in red curry paste can be served as a main dish or along with other dishes to create a complete Thai menu. Once you master this simple stir-fry, you will find yourself serving it in a variety of ways. You can use the vegetables listed below or substitute your favorites. This recipe can be prepared with fresh or frozen vegetables (preferably organic).

Serves 4 to 6

Ingredients

4 medium carrots

½ pound green beans

1 small red bell pepper

1 can sliced bamboo shoots

4 ounces fresh or frozen corn (about ½ cup)

3 green onions

1 small bunch fresh basil

2 shallots

1 to 2 tablespoons red curry paste (page 63)

¼ cup cold water

2 tablespoons granulated sugar

2 tablespoons soy sauce

3 tablespoons vegetable oil

On your mark . . .

- Wash and peel the carrots.

- Cut the carrots in half lengthwise and lay the flat side down on the cutting board.

- Cut the halves into long strips and then cut the strips into 3-inch-long pieces. Measure 1 to 1 ½ cups, place in a bowl, and set to the side.

- Wash the green beans and remove the stems and tips.

- Slice into 3-inch pieces. Measure 1 to 1 ½ cups and add to the carrots.

- Wash the bell pepper, cut it in half, and remove the seeds.

- Cut each half into long strips. Cut each strip into pieces about the size of the carrots and add to the bowl.

- Open the bamboo shoots and pour the can into a hand strainer or colander.

- Rinse with cold water for at least 30 seconds, then add to the bowl.

- If using fresh corn, cut the kernels off the cob with a knife, turning the cob after each cut. Measure ½ cup and set aside.

- If using frozen corn, measure ½ cup and add to the bowl.

- Wash the green onions and remove and discard any dark or discolored outer leaves.

- Cut off the root end and discard. Cut the green onions into ¼-inch slices and add to the vegetables.

- Wash the basil leaves and shake off any excess water. Remove the leaves and discard the stems, measure ¼ cup, and set aside for garnish.

- Peel the shallots, slice into thin rings, and set aside.

Get set . . .

- Place the vegetables, curry paste, water, sugar, and soy sauce next to the stove.

Cook!

- Add the oil to a wok or 10- to 12-inch frying pan and place over medium-high heat for 30 seconds.

- Add the sliced shallots and fry them for 2 to 3 minutes, or until they are slightly crispy.

- Remove them to a plate lined with a paper towel and set aside.

- Reheat the oil again for 20 to 30 seconds and add the curry paste. Fry for 1 to 2 minutes.

- Add the water and stir until combined and the curry paste has thinned a little.

- Add all the vegetables, sugar, and soy sauce, and stir-fry for 5 to 6 minutes, or until the vegetables are just tender.

- Arrange them on a serving platter, garnish with the reserved basil leaves and crispy shallots, and serve with rice.

Sweet Pork *Moo-Wan*

Here is a simple recipe from the north of Thailand that turns pork tenderloin into sweet perfection. Serve it as a main course with rice or alongside cucumber relish (page 35), pickled vegetables (page 43), or shrimp in coconut cream (page 71). However you serve it, watch out. You might find yourself sneaking back to eat any leftovers—if someone else hasn't already beaten you to it.

Serves 4 to 6

Ingredients

3 shallots

1 pound pork tenderloin

3 tablespoons vegetable oil

¾ cup dark brown sugar

1 tablespoon soy sauce

3 tablespoons Thai fish sauce

¼ cup water

½ teaspoon ground white pepper

On your mark, get set . . .

- Peel and cut the shallots into thin slices, measure ½ cup, and set aside.

- Remove any fat or skin from the outside of the tenderloin and discard.

- Cut the pork into ¼-inch-thick slices and set aside.

Cook!

- Add the oil to a wok or 10-inch frying pan and place over medium-high heat for about 1 minute.

- Add the shallots and stir-fry for 1 to 2 minutes, or until the shallots begin to turn brown and crispy.

- Add the sugar and stir until melted; be careful not to splash yourself.

- Add the soy sauce, fish sauce, water, and white pepper and bring to a boil.

- Add the pork, reduce the heat to medium, and cook for 5 to 6 minutes, or until the pork is tender and cooked through.

- Once the pork is cooked, remove it with a slotted spoon to a heatproof bowl.

- Turn the heat to high and boil the sauce for 1 minute to reduce and thicken it.

- Pour the sauce over the pork and serve hot with rice.

Shrimp in Coconut Cream
Lhon Goon

If you think that all Thai cooking is spicy, you are in for a real surprise when you first try shrimp in coconut cream. This dish is traditionally served along with an assortment of pickled vegetables (page 43) or with sweet pork (page 69). This recipe, originally from the royal family of King Rama II, is regarded by many as a classic example of just how elegant Thai food can be.

Serves 4

Ingredients

6 large shrimp

¼ pound ground pork (about 3 tablespoons)

1 red jalapeño chile

3 to 4 sprigs cilantro

2 shallots

1 cup canned unsweetened coconut milk

½ cup homemade chicken stock (page 22) or canned low-sodium chicken broth

1 teaspoon light brown sugar

1 teaspoon salt

On your mark, get set . . .

- Peel and discard the shells and the tails of the shrimp.

- Remove the vein from the shrimp. To do this, lay the shrimp on a cutting board. Using a paring knife, make a slight cut about ¼ inch deep, starting at the widest end, or the top of the shrimp and continuing down the back.

- Gently open the back along the cut, and you will see a black vein.

- Rinse the shrimp under cold running water, then pull out and discard the vein.

- Repeat with the rest of the shrimp.

- Finely chop the shrimp into small pieces and place in a small bowl.

- Add the ground pork to the shrimp and, using a fork, mash them together into a thick paste.

- Slip on a pair of kitchen gloves. Cut the chile in half and remove the stem. To remove the seeds, rinse the chile under cold running water and scrape out the seeds with the tip of a teaspoon and discard.

- Dice or finely chop the chile, measure 1 tablespoon, and set aside.

- Rinse, dry, and remove the gloves.

- Rinse the cilantro to remove any dirt or sand, shake off the excess water, and pat dry with paper towels. Remove the leaves and discard the stems. Roughly chop the leaves and set aside.

- Peel the outer skin from the shallots.

- Slice the shallots into thin rings, measure 2 tablespoons, and set aside.

Cook!

- Combine the coconut milk, chicken stock, light brown sugar, and salt in a 3- to 4-quart saucepan. Bring to a boil over medium-high heat.

- Add the shrimp-and-pork combination.

- Return the pan to a boil, then reduce the heat to low.

- Stir the shrimp-and-pork combination to break it up. Cook for 3 to 4 minutes.

- Add the shallots, cilantro, and chile, cook for 1 minute, and remove from the heat.

- Serve with fresh or pickled vegetables (page 43).

Grilled Chicken with Sweet-Heat Sauce
Gai Yang Lath Nam-thim

There is an endless assortment of tantalizing foods sold on the streets of Thailand. *Gai yang*, or "grilled chicken," is certainly one of the most famous. This recipe is usually cooked over charcoal. If you decide to barbecue, you will need your adult assistant to help you with the grilling. This recipe, however, can be prepared entirely in the oven with very tasty results.

Serves 4

Ingredients

THE MARINADE

1 3 ½- to 4-pound chicken cut into 8 to 10 pieces, preferably organic

2 garlic cloves

1 serrano chile

6 to 7 stems cilantro

2 tablespoons hot chili sesame oil

3 tablespoons Thai fish sauce

1 tablespoon sugar

THE SWEET-HEAT SAUCE

1 garlic clove

1 to 2 jalapeño (red or green) or serrano chiles

¼ cup rice wine vinegar

¼ cup sugar

1 teaspoon salt

On your mark . . .

- Wash the chicken and cut it into 8 to 10 pieces.

- Dry each piece with a paper towel and place in a large bowl. Peel and chop the garlic and place it in a small bowl.

- Chop the chile and add it to the same bowl.

- Wash the cilantro and shake off the excess water. Remove the leaves and save for another recipe.

- Chop the stems and combine them with the rest of the ingredients for the marinade in a small bowl. Mix well to combine.

- Pour over the chicken, toss with a large spoon to coat all the pieces, and refrigerate for at least 2 hours or overnight.
- While marinating, take a spoon and occasionally recoat the chicken pieces with the liquid to distribute the flavor more evenly.

Get set . . .

- Peel and chop the garlic. Chop the chile, and set both aside.
- Pour the vinegar, sugar, and salt into a small saucepan, and place it over medium heat.
- Cook for about 3 minutes, or until the vinegar thickens and the sugar is melted.
- If the vinegar begins to boil, reduce the heat.
- Pour the sauce into a bowl and cool for 10 minutes.
- Add the chopped garlic and chiles.
- Set the sauce aside until ready to serve the chicken.

Cook!

- Preheat the oven to 450°F.
- Completely cover a 10 ½ x 14-inch baking pan with aluminum foil. This will help with cleanup later. If using a nonstick baking pan, there is no need to cover it with foil.
- Place a baking rack, lightly brushed with oil to prevent sticking, inside the baking dish. The rack should be large enough to hold all the pieces of chicken in a single layer.
- Remove the chicken pieces from the marinade and place them on the rack.
- Brush the remaining marinade evenly over the chicken pieces.
- Place the pan on the middle rack of the oven and bake the chicken for 25 minutes.
- After 25 minutes, reduce the heat to 375°F and bake for 35 to 40 minutes, or until the chicken is crispy, browned, and cooked through to the bone.
- Serve hot with the sweet-heat sauce.

Chef's Tip #1

Marinating the chicken gives it its flavor. Plan ahead so you have at least 2 hours to marinate the meat, or preferably overnight. The results are well worth the extra time spent.

Chef's Tip #2

Red jalapeño chiles are generally milder than the green variety.

Grilled Chicken with Peanut Sauce
Satay Gai

This recipe is commonly associated with Thai cooking, though it probably came from Malaysia. *Satay* is a Chinese word that means "three pieces." Grilled chicken with peanut sauce is a wonderful example of how three different and delicious Thai dishes blend into one. This version comes from the south and is similar to the satay of the central region. The "three pieces" here are grilled marinated chicken, peanut sauce, and cucumber relish. But the only word you will remember is awesome.

Serves 4

Ingredients

THE CHICKEN

1 to 1 ½ pounds skinless boneless chicken breasts, preferably organic

18 bamboo skewers

THE MARINADE

½ cup canned unsweetened coconut milk

2 tablespoons peanut or vegetable oil

2 tablespoons granulated sugar

1 teaspoon salt

½ teaspoon ground coriander

½ teaspoon ground cumin

½ teaspoon turmeric

1 teaspoon curry powder

1 to 2 limes

5 to 6 whole lettuce leaves—Boston, butter, or head lettuce

1 recipe cucumber relish (page 35)

THE PEANUT SAUCE

½ cup homemade chicken stock (page 22) or canned low-sodium chicken broth

½ cup unsweetened coconut milk

1 tablespoon red curry paste (page 63), depending on taste

1 teaspoon Thai fish sauce

2 tablespoons granulated sugar

½ cup chunky or smooth peanut butter, preferably all natural

2 tablespoons plain bread crumbs

On your mark . . .

- Wash the chicken breasts and pat dry with paper towels.

- Remove any skin or fat from the outside.

- Place the chicken breasts on a clean plate, cover loosely with aluminum foil, and partially freeze for 15 to 20 minutes to make slicing them easier. Set a timer so you won't forget.

- In a large bowl, combine the coconut milk, oil, sugar, salt, ground coriander, cumin, turmeric, and curry powder.

- Mix well with a whisk to combine all the ingredients for the marinade.

Get set . . .

- Remove the chicken from the freezer.

- Slice each breast lengthwise into very thin strips.

- Each slice should be about 3 inches long and 1 ½ inches wide.

- You will need a total of 36 chicken strips.

- Take one strip of chicken and lay it flat on a clean cutting board.

- Place the tip of the skewer underneath the end of the chicken strip closest to you. Push the skewer about 1 inch into the meat and then out the top of the strip.

- Push the tip of the skewer back into and under the strip and finish by pulling the skewer out the top of the strip. Stand the skewer on end and gently press the meat down the skewer to make room for a second piece of chicken.

- Repeat this step with a second strip of chicken on the same skewer.

- Lay the skewered strips on a clean plate. Repeat with the rest of the chicken until all the skewers are filled with two pieces per skewer.

- Place one layer of the chicken strips into a glass or stainless-steel dish large enough to hold all the skewers.

- Spoon some of the marinade over the first layer of skewers to evenly coat the chicken.

- Place another layer over the top and spoon on the remainder of the marinade.

- Refrigerate for 1 to 2 hours or overnight.

- After the chicken strips have marinated, squeeze the juice from the lime, measure 2 tablespoons, and set aside.

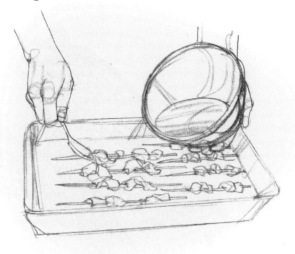

- Wash the lettuce leaves, shake off the excess water, wrap in a paper towel, and refrigerate.

Cook!

- Put the chicken stock and coconut milk in a 2- to 3-quart saucepan over medium heat.

- Slowly bring to a boil, stirring it a few times. Add the curry paste and mix well until it dissolves and the liquid changes color.

- Add the sugar, peanut butter, and bread crumbs.

- Reduce the heat to simmer and cook for 2 to 3 minutes, stirring frequently.

- Remove from the heat, add the reserved lime juice, cool for 10 minutes, and refrigerate.

- When you are ready to cook the chicken strips, ask your adult assistant to help with the next step.

- Place a broiler pan on the highest rack in the oven.

- Turn the broiler on and preheat for 2 to 3 minutes.

- Broil the chicken skewers for 2 to 3 minutes on each side, turning once with tongs, until they are lightly browned and starting to crisp. You may have to do the broiling in a couple of batches.

- Lay the broiled chicken strips on a serving platter lined with the chilled lettuce leaves.

- Place the sauce in a serving bowl on the platter along with the cucumber relish.

- Invite your guests to dip the chicken into the peanut sauce and enjoy along with some of the relish.

Banana cake (left)
and baked coconut
custard.

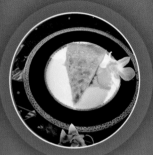

Desserts

Baked Coconut Custard
Kanom Mur Geang

Phetchaburi is a city to the southwest of Bangkok. Sugar palms grow in abundance there. So it is not surprising the town has a reputation for its outstanding desserts. This custard is an adaptation of a dish that started off being sold from a street vendor's cart in the town. Eventually the custard became so popular that a national chain of shops now sells it all over Thailand. You just never know where a good dessert might take you.

Serves 4

Ingredients

1 cup dried yellow split peas

3 cups water

1 teaspoon butter

1 teaspoon flour

1 cup canned unsweetened coconut cream

½ cup canned unsweetened coconut milk

½ cup heavy cream

2 cups granulated sugar

3 eggs

On your mark, get set . . .

- Pour the split peas into a large bowl. Check the peas for any small stones or debris and remove them.

- Fill the bowl with cold water and, using your very clean hands, swirl the peas around to wash them.

- Drain the water carefully, pour the split peas into a 4-quart pot, add the 3 cups water, and place on the stove.

- Make sure the cover of the pot is close by.

Cook!

- Bring the split peas to a boil over high heat uncovered. This will take about 15 minutes.

- Reduce the heat to simmer, cover the pot, and cook for 35 to 40 minutes, or until very tender.

- In the meantime, butter the inside of a 9 ½ x 2-inch round cake pan or oval baking dish, evenly coating the bottom and sides.

- Add the flour and tip the pan back and forth to evenly cover the entire surface. Tap out the excess flour and set aside.

- When the split peas are tender, drain in a colander and let cool for 15 to 20 minutes.

- Preheat the oven to 350°F.

- Make sure the peas have cooled completely; if the peas are still hot, you will start cooking the raw eggs.

- Pour the cooled split peas in a large bowl and, using an electric hand mixer, beat them on low for 1 minute, or until they are smooth and lightened in color.

- Open the canned coconut milk and, using a spoon, lift off the thick cream at the top of the can. Measure 1 cup and add to the bowl with the cooked peas. Blend until smooth.

- Now add the heavy cream, coconut milk, and sugar and beat for another 1 or 2 minutes.

- Add the eggs, one at a time, blending each one until it is fully mixed into the custard.

- Pour the custard into the baking pan and bake on the middle rack of the oven for 60 to 65 minutes, or until the custard is firm and golden brown around the edges.

- Remove from the oven, place on a cooling rack, and let cool to room temperature.

- Cover with aluminum foil and chill completely.

- To serve, cut into thin slices and serve cold.

Chef's Tip

Coconut cream comes in cans sold in many supermarkets. If it is unavailable, use a total of 1 ½ cups coconut milk.

Banana Cake *Kanom Gluay*

Bananas grow in abundance in the hot and humid climate of southern Thailand, where there are more than a dozen varieties to choose from. Thai cooks deep-fry them, make them into custards, and even slow cook them in coconut milk. Here is an adaptation of a classic recipe for a wonderfully rich banana-and-coconut cake. Traditionally this recipe is steamed in a wok, but this version allows you to bake it. The results are delicious just the same.

Serves 4

Ingredients

2 ¼ cups unsweetened shredded coconut

1 ¼ cups cold water

½ teaspoon soft, unsalted butter

1 cup cake flour plus 1 tablespoon for dusting baking pan

5 ripe bananas

¼ cup cold cooked white rice, preferably

Thai jasmine or basmati

¾ cup canned unsweetened coconut cream

3 eggs

1 ¾ cups granulated sugar

½ cup canned coconut milk

2 tablespoons confectioners' sugar

On your mark . . .

- Place the coconut in a large bowl with the water and let it soak for 10 minutes.

- After 10 minutes, drain the coconut in a strainer and, using the back of a large spoon, squeeze out the water.

- Remove ¼ cup of the drained coconut and set it aside for garnishing the cake after it has baked.

- Lightly grease a 10 x 2-inch round baking pan with the butter.

- Add the tablespoon of flour and tip the baking pan back and forth until the entire surface is lightly coated.

- Tap out the excess flour and discard.

- Set the baking pan aside and be careful not to touch the inside of it once you have buttered and floured it.

Get set . . .

- Preheat the oven to 350°F.

- Return the remaining drained coconut to the bowl.

- Peel the bananas, remove and discard the dark tips at the top and bottom, cut into 2-inch slices, measure 2 to 2 ½ cups, and place them in the bowl along with the coconut and rice.

- To obtain the coconut cream, open a can of coconut milk and, using a spoon, lift off the thick cream at the top of the can.

- Add the coconut cream to the bowl with the bananas.

- Using a potato masher, mash the coconut, bananas, rice, and coconut cream until well combined. This will take a few minutes, so be patient.

- Set the banana mixture aside for a moment.

- Break the eggs into a medium bowl and add the sugar.

- Beat with an electric hand mixer on high for 2 minutes until light and foamy.

Cook!

- Add about ⅓ of the eggs to the banana mixture along with ⅓ of the remaining flour.

- Using the electric hand mixer on medium, blend the ingredients together.
- Add the next ⅓ of the eggs and flour and continue to blend.
- Add the remaining eggs and flour and blend into a smooth batter.
- Turn off the mixer. Add the ½ cup of coconut milk, and, using a rubber spatula, blend it into the batter.
- Pour the cake batter into the baking pan and place on the center rack of the oven.
- Bake for 60 to 65 minutes, or until the cake is lightly browned and a knife inserted in the center comes out clean with no batter clinging to it.
- Cool the cake on a wire rack for 10 minutes.
- Sprinkle with the remaining shredded coconut and the confectioners' sugar.
- Let cool to room temperature, cut into small pieces, and serve.

Chef's Tip

It is important that the bananas are ripe for this recipe, so plan ahead. A ripe banana is one with brown spots that has softened. Look for the different varieties that are available in supermarkets and add those to the cake; just make sure they have ripened.

Helpful Kitchen Equipment and Utensils

BAKING PAN

CAKE PAN

COFFEE GRINDER

FOOD PROCESSOR

WOK

FOUR-SIDED GRATER

MIXING BOWL

SPATULA

COLANDER

KNIVES, ASSORTED

LARGE METAL SPOON

STOCKPOT

COOKIE SHEETS

LADLE

JUICER

STRAINER

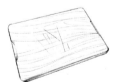

CUTTING BOARD

MORTAR AND PESTLE

SAUCEPANS WITH LIDS, ASSORTED SIZES

VEGETABLE PEELER

ELECTRIC MIXER

ROASTING PAN

SKILLETS

WHISK

Bamboo Shoots

These are the young edible shoots of the bamboo tree. They are harvested as soon as they make their first appearance above ground. Delicate with a nutty flavor, fresh bamboo shoots can be found in Asian specialty markets. For convenience, they are also available canned. Once you open the can, rinse the shoots under cold water to remove any bitter flavor. They are already cooked, so canned bamboo shoots are perfect for fast-cooking, stir-fried dishes. Once opened, they will keep for about two weeks in a closed container of fresh water. The water should be changed two or three times per week to ensure freshness.

Basil

Look for fresh basil that is bright in color and has no dark spots. Use only the leaves and not the stems. There are many varieties to choose from including red or opal, holy basil, lemon basil, or basil with red stems and green leaves, which is called Thai basil. Basil leaves can hold dirt. Wash them well, then pat them dry. The best way to use basil is not to cut it with a knife, but tear it with your fingers instead. This will ensure that you don't bruise it and create dark spots.

Chile Garlic Sauce

Chile garlic sauce is available in most supermarkets.

Chile Peppers, Dried

Dried chile peppers are an essential part of Thai cooking. Dried chiles offer a greater variety of chiles to choose from than what is available fresh. For the recipes in this book, look for New Mexico, California, or *chile de arbol*, usually available in the produce sections of most supermarkets.

Chile Peppers, Fresh

Jalapeño peppers are an excellent substitute for authentic Thai peppers. Jalapeños are green or red in color, with the red being generally milder. Serrano peppers have become very popular in Thai cooking. They are about 2 inches long (a bit smaller than the jalapeño) and are bullet shaped. It is important when handling chiles, dried or fresh, to wear latex kitchen gloves and to wash and dry the gloves after you are done handling the chiles. Never touch your eyes, nose, or any other part of your face to prevent contact with hot oils that are naturally found in chiles.

Cilantro

Cilantro is an herb also known as fresh coriander or Chinese parsley. It adds great flavor to Thai dishes. The Thai cook loves cilantro. Not only are the leaves and stems used in cooking, but so is the root. Cilantro looks almost identical to parsley and is easily confused with it, but it has a bolder flavor and a strong aroma. Cilantro should be washed to remove any dirt still clinging to the stems or leaves. Wrapped in paper towel and then plastic, it will keep for about a week in the refrigerator.

Coconut Milk

Coconut milk is a common ingredient in Thai cooking. There are a few different types of milk to choose from when preparing the recipes in this book. Many people are concerned about the fat content of coconut milk and select a "lite" or "ultra-lite" version. The choice is yours, and any of the varieties will work. When buying coconut milk, avoid shaking the can. That way the cream will be at the top when it is opened, and you can remove it with a spoon to use in the recipe. Canned unsweetened coconut cream is also available, and its fat content, like real cream, is higher than that of milk.

Curry Powder

This popular blend of spices and herbs is commonly associated with India and the United Kingdom, not Thailand. Many years ago, several Indian spices were blended together by Indian cooks at the request of British subjects returning home. The idea was that when they wanted a taste of India, they simply used the spice mixture to remind them of the pleasures of Indian cooking they had left behind.

Fish Sauce

Fish sauce is an essential ingredient in the cooking of Southeast Asia, and its flavor clearly identifies a dish as Thai or Vietnamese. The sauce is created from small fish that are first pounded, then packed in earthenware jars with salt and roasted rice, then wrapped in banana leaves and fermented in the sun. Look for fish sauce that has a light, almost clear or amber color. Once opened, it will have a strong aroma of fish and a salty taste. However, after it is added to a recipe, its subtle flavor blends. Refrigerate it after you open it, and discard it after the liquid turns cloudy.

Galangal or Ginger

Fresh galangal is a type of young ginger that grows in the Tropics. It has a taste that combines ginger, lemon, and pepper. It can be found in

Asian specialty markets. If you can't find it, you can substitute the more common ginger, which is another important flavoring agent in Thailand. When you shop for fresh ginger, look for a nice smooth skin with no dark spots. Peel off the outer skin with a potato peeler, then slice off the amount the recipe calls for with a sharp knife. Tightly wrap the remaining piece in plastic wrap and refrigerate. Fresh ginger will keep in the refrigerator for up to two weeks. A grater also works to help get the juice out of it.

Garlic

Garlic is a member of the onion family and a valuable flavor maker in Thai cooking. When you purchase garlic, look for large bulbs that are hard and solid. Inside the bulb are cloves. To use the cloves, first separate them from the bulb. With the flat side of a knife, give them a good whack, then remove the white paperlike skin and cut off the dark tip. The cloves can be chopped into small pieces, mashed, or cut into thin slices. Many nutritionists believe that garlic has great health benefits because it is rich in minerals.

Green Curry Paste

Green curry paste is available in most supermarkets usually in the specialty foods section. The combination of ingredients may vary, but usually the paste contains ginger or galangal, lemongrass, hot green chiles, lime zest, coriander root, basil, garlic, and shrimp paste. The color may be green, but the flavor is hot. Use it according to your own taste.

Lemongrass

This tall grass plant grows in abundance in Thailand and is an important ingredient in countless dishes. You may find it in the produce section of large supermarkets or in Asian food markets. It resembles a green onion except its outer skin is tough and stringy. To use lemongrass, peel away the tough outer layers to reveal light purple rings inside. If you slice off the root end and give it a sniff, you will discover where its name comes from by its lemon aroma. Sliced thin or cut in larger pieces and crushed, lemongrass will keep wrapped in the refrigerator for about three weeks.

Miso

Miso, or bean paste, consists of soybeans fermented with rice, barley, wheat, or rye. Originally from China, but now popular all over, miso is a favorite ingredient in vegetarian cooking because it provides protein and flavor to meatless dishes. Keep it refrigerated and check the expiration date when purchasing it. Choose the date that is the furthest from the date when you are buying it.

Papaya

Papayas grow abundantly in the hot and humid climate of Thailand. They are eaten both ripe and underripe or green. The most common papaya available in Western supermarkets come from Hawaii and weigh about 1 pound. When shopping for underripe papayas, look for ones that are and green without any dark spots. When shopping for ripe papaya, look for one that is soft, with a light yellow color and no dark spots.

Red Curry Paste
Red curry paste is available in supermarkets, or you can follow the recipe on page 63 to make your own. A blend of spices, ginger, chile peppers, shrimp paste, and lemongrass, red curry paste is one of Thailand's milder pastes. It is still hot, though, so use it according to your own taste.

Rice Noodles, Dried
Rice noodles are available in supermarkets or health food stores. Rice noodles are first soaked in water before they are quickly cooked. Watch them carefully as they cook and taste them frequently to make sure they don't over- or undercook. You know they are done when they still have a little slightly firm bite to them and are not yet too soft.

Shallots
These delicate, small bulbs belong to the onion family. Their flavor is milder than garlic, but their appearance is similar. Thai cooks use them in place of onions and prefer a variety that is red. The flavor of the shallot is released when it is cooked. Shallots should be stored in a cool, dry place out of the sun. They should remain fresh for a few weeks after you purchase them.

Shrimp Paste
Shrimp paste is made from fermented shrimp. The paste is intensely flavored and is a common ingredient in curries. It is worth seeing if there is an Asian market in your area where you can purchase it. If not, you can substitute bean paste, also called miso.

Tofu
Made from soybeans, tofu is a wonderful source of protein. By itself, plain tofu has very little flavor, but it has the ability to absorb the flavors of the other ingredients in a dish. Tofu is also available in a variety of new flavors and textures. It is sold in soft, medium, firm, or extra-firm cakes. Check your recipe to see which type is right for your dish. Tofu comes packed in water and must be kept refrigerated. When you get it home, remove it from the container and rinse it. Place it in a jar, add fresh water, and then cover and refrigerate it. Change the water every day to keep the tofu from turning sour, and use it within a week.

Find Out More/Metric Conversion Chart

Books

Krummer, Patricia K. *The Food of Thailand* (Flavors of the World). Tarrytown, NY: Marshall Cavendish Benchmark, 2012.

McDermott, Nancie. *Quick & Easy Thai*. San Francisco: Chronicle Books, 2004.

Rau, Dana Meachen. *Thailand*. Tarrytown, NY: Marshall Cavendish Benchmark, 2007.

Websites

Thai Cooking for Kids
http://www.supatra.com/pages/thaicookingkids.html
Features information about Thai food and cooking, as well as easy-to-prepare recipes.

Learn Thai Culture
http://www.learnthaiculture.com
Learn all about Thai culture, traditions, customs, and more.

Metric Conversion Chart

You can use the chart below to convert from U.S. measurements to the metric system.

Weight
1 ounce = 28 grams
½ pound (8 ounces) = 227 grams
1 pound = .45 kilogram
2.2 pounds = 1 kilogram

Liquid volume
1 teaspoon = 5 milliliters
1 tablespoon = 15 milliliters
1 fluid ounce = 30 milliliters
1 cup = 240 milliliters (.24 liter)
1 pint = 480 milliliters (.48 liter)
1 quart = .95 liter

Length
¼ inch = .6 centimeter
½ inch = 1.25 centimeters
1 inch = 2.5 centimeters

Temperature
100°F = 40°C
110°F = 45°C
212°F = 100°C (boiling point of water)
350°F = 180°C
375°F = 190°C
400°F = 200°C
425°F = 220°C
450°F = 235°C

(To convert temperatures in Fahrenheit to Celsius, subtract 32 and multiply by .56)

Index

Page numbers in **boldface** are photographs.

Chef Matthew Locricchio knows a thing or two about cooking. What sets this chef apart from other talented professionals in his field is his knack for imparting this culinary wisdom to children. Matthew was born in Michigan and into a restaurant and catering family, and has spent most of his life in the food industry. Along with his years of training as a chef and his numerous books on cooking, Matthew has made guest appearances on Martha Stewart Radio, *Everyday Food* to talk about his unique approach to getting kids interested in cooking. He has also been heard on *The Faith Middleton Show: Food Schmooze*, on National Public Radio (NPR), and seen on WGN TV, *Lunch Break*, in Chicago.

Matthew's award-winning *The 2nd International Cookbook for Kids* followed up on his earlier *The International Cookbook for Kids*, and, much like the first book, is full of delicious, kid-friendly recipes from around the world.

Also a playwright and actor, Matthew has worked in numerous commercials, soap operas, films, and television shows. Chef Locricchio has been a guest instructor at The Institute of Culinary Education in New York City and Stonewall Kitchen in York, Maine. He guest lectures in the series "Adventures in the Global Kitchen for Kids and Families" at The American Museum of Natural History in New York City.

His brand new *Teen Cuisine*, with spectacular photos by James Beard Winner, James Peterson, was released October 1, 2010. He is currently writing a follow-up with a vegetarian cookbook.

More information about Matthew Locricchio can be found at his website: www.cookbooksandkids.com or www.teencuisinebooks.com